Out of th

Out of the Desert

Mike Dwight

New Wine Press

Printed in the United Kingdom

Dedication

I would like to dedicate this book to my wife, best friend and co-worker, Wilma, who has encouraged and sharpened me in so many ways and continues to be a great support. Also to our children, Paul, Esther and Karen, who have been very much part of the journey and are such a joy to us. I am very grateful for the privilege of working in Thailand and other parts of Asia for over 35 years. The Thai people will always have a special place in my heart and the WEC Thailand team graciously gave me the opportunity to serve with them. Finally, to WEC Betel for giving me the freedom to serve in Asia and Europe; without their encouragement this book would never have been written.

Contents

Foreword

I have known Mike Dwight since he began his journey with Jesus, and have followed that journey with prayer and gratitude. At the beginning of Chapter 9 Mike says, 'What I have shared in this book is not the product of study so much as an opening of my heart to what God has personally been doing in me over these past few years.' I think that is an accurate description of its contents, although there is a depth, an insight, and an understanding of Scripture that belies a lifetime of study. Mike certainly encourages us to walk with him on his own personal pilgrimage and courageously unveils his humanity with intrusive integrity.

The book is based on a series of addresses that Mike gave at a Spanish conference. That can often be a recipe for disaster, but not this time. The spoken word has been wonderfully communicated as the written word. Is this simply because of the author's openness and humility? I have no doubt that this plays a part, but there is another dimension to its contents – the unmistakeable anointing of the Spirit of God. It is impossible to read it without being deeply challenged, not by Mike Dwight but by the Lord Himself. It has caused me to ponder, reflect and examine my own spirituality. My own life has been challenged, and hopefully changed, as a result of its contents. In the Introduction, Mike says, 'there is so much more to God, and I wonder if you and I will be part of discovering and experiencing that truth?'

This is no ivory-tower attempt to write a book. It is written by someone who has heard the Call of God, followed directions to equip and prepare himself to answer that Call, been engrossed in mission to the unreached in a culture unfamiliar to him, and in these later years travelled widely in different countries and continents to share the passion of his heart. However, beneath all that 'exterior' activity there has increasingly been a heart hungry to know God better, to feel His heartbeat, to know His agenda, to become more familiar with His ways, and to give God what He has always been looking for – not only for him but for us too! What else could explain his conclusion that his biblical hero is Enoch (the man who 'walked with God')? Just so!! The Bible describes angels as created to be God's servants, but we have been created for intimacy and fellowship with Him. How often in our busyness have we missed the longing of God's heart?

Personal testimony constantly emerges from its pages, and this is interspersed with encouragement to reflect on Scripture and on the movement of God in different parts of the world and in the lives of individuals. The whole book is anchored in the Book of Exodus and the personal lessons that are to be learned from the life of Moses – a Somebody who had to become a Nobody in order to show us all what God can do with a Nobody making him into His Somebody!

This is not so much a book to be enjoyed as to be experienced.

Jim Graham, Pastor Emeritus at Gold Hill
Baptist Church, Chalfont St Peter

Introduction

This book started life as a set of talks I gave in August 2013 centred around Exodus 33 and God's planned journey for Moses and the people. I had the privilege of speaking at the annual WEC Betel Conference in Spain. Betel is involved in a worldwide mission rescuing broken and addicted lives, planting churches and impacting communities for Christ. It started in San Blas, Spain, in 1986 and is now working in 23 countries.

Betel's development and current growth is a 'modern day Acts' type adventure. It combines simple yet costly obedience, faith, passion, vision and trust in God who has revealed Himself perfectly in His Son Jesus Christ. As a result of His death, resurrection, ascension and glorification to the Father's right hand, Christ has poured out the Holy Spirit's power into frail, messed up and very ordinary people.

Today he loves to repeat this over and over again. This privilege brings with it a mandate to take the good news of Jesus Christ to a world which has never heard that He alone is Saviour and Lord.

Though these messages were originally for the Betel worldwide context, Elliott Tepper, the international director and founder of WEC Betel, and others felt that they were relevant for the wider church and also for the many challenges mission organisations are facing worldwide.

MJD, January 2015

CHAPTER 1

Going down a new road

As I write this I am in Ulaanbaatar, the capital of Mongolia. Yesterday I went out into the countryside. It was an amazing day. The first winter snow had fallen, the sun was shining and there was not a cloud in the sky. The mountain scenery was stunning, beautiful and unspoilt. The air was breathtakingly fresh, so different from the humid life in Bangkok, Thailand, where we live.

The road we travelled on was for me a journey into the unknown. I have always longed to see an eagle flying in the wild. I remember many years ago having a holiday with my brothers on the Isle of Arran hoping to see an eagle soaring over Goat Fell, Arran's highest mountain at 874 meters or 2866 feet. (Arran is an island off the west coast of Scotland.) Alas that dream was not fulfilled.

And now here I am on an unfamiliar road amid the eagles of Mongolia. My friends had been on this road many times before but for me it was a brand new journey. This book is about a current challenge and journey that many in the past have travelled on. They have had their hope restored, their strength renewed and have soared as on eagles' wings (Isaiah 40:31). We have admired their story, been thrilled by their testimony and experience, and been filled with awe as they enjoyed the privilege of being in what A. W. Tozer calls the 'manifest Presence of God'. God is calling us to travel on that road for ourselves.

Apart from Elliott's personal encouragement, this book most importantly reflects the personal challenge of the Spirit of God both to me and, I believe, to the church and mission world in this critical moment of opportunity and advance, with 25–27% of the world still waiting to hear the Good News of Jesus. The challenge to go on God's journey, whether for Moses or for us today, will impact us all in different ways. For a large worldwide mission like WEC International, founded by C.T. Studd in 1913, now with around 1800 workers from 50 countries serving in multicultural teams among nearly 100 unreached people groups, the challenge is greater than just increasing the number of workers or becoming more flexible in order to reach the unreached with the Gospel.

However, this book could also be relevant to:

- the different stages in your personal life and walk with God
- the specific challenges and opportunities at a church level
- or you may be at a crossroad point in mission, and preparing for the next stage of God's journey, reaching the unreached areas of the world.

Our spiritual lives can become settled and comfortable. We can get locked into a convenient routine of managing our daily, weekly walk with God that can look reasonable to all around us, but does not satisfy that deeper longing for the renewing, reviving presence of the Spirit. A fresh revelation of this is often necessary as God causes us to face up to the next stage of His journey for us.

This revelation breaks into our settled comfortable routines with an awareness that there is so much more to God than we are currently aware, but also with a doubt: 'I wonder if I will be part of discovering and experiencing this truth and the "much more" of God?'

Brazil 2008

In 2008 I was in Brazil for meetings with the senior leadership of WEC from around the world, about 25 of us altogether. A local pastor came and shared in one of the devotional meetings from 2 Kings 4: Elisha and the widow's oil. During this message he brought a simple word of prophecy that was to have a huge impact on my life both then and even now today.

He saw a picture of a jumbo jet circling around an airfield desperately wanting to land. This plane was full of God's gifts: new supplies of His grace, love, freedom, revelation and truth and a fresh sense of His Presence and Glory; however, the plane was unable to land.

The runway had become overgrown, the tarmac broken and full of holes. Around the airport people were busy and active, trying desperately to bring help to the people in need. In their busyness they were oblivious to the plane circling overhead with God's fresh supplies, the need to repair and prepare the runway, and their personal, desperate situation and need of God.

This prophetic word began a creative work of change in me which was so obviously needed. My comfortable, spiritual, missionary world had been invaded by the Spirit of God. The automatic mode of life and ministry which probably appeared impressive to my colleagues now seemed so dissatisfying. My vision had been changed in that moment from sincere mission activity to repairing the runway for a new visitation from God.

I realised that in the special moments when God is so close, the past – no matter how good – cannot satisfy that freshly revived hunger to discover more of His Presence and Glory.

Chapter 2

What stage of the journey are we looking at?

> *God is calling us to travel on this new road*

Then the LORD said to Moses, 'Leave this place, you and the people you brought up out of Egypt, and go up to the land I promised on oath to Abraham, Isaac and Jacob, saying, "I will give it to your descendants" ' (Exodus 33:1).

The exodus out of Egypt at this point seemed a long while ago to the Israelites. Would they ever get out of the desert? God's promise to Moses and the people was that He would not only lead them out of Egypt and free them from Pharaoh, but lead them into the land He had promised to Abraham. The word from God in Exodus 33 shows that it is time to move on.

My intention as we explore this journey is not to leave us looking at the courageous acts of faith undertaken by man, although that would be valuable, challenging and beneficial. It is, however, to recapture the heart-pounding awareness of the nearness and supernatural reality of God Himself walking with men in day-to-day life, and His challenge to move towards a new place of life and ministry.

The Moravians

As I refer to the reality of God walking with men in day-to-day life I can't help but think back to the Moravians. They were led by Nicolas Von Zinzendorf (1700–1760) and originated in Germany. On 25 August 1727 a prayer meeting started that lasted 24/7 for over 100 years. During this time there was an incredible sense of God's Spirit released in a supernatural way. Over the coming years, from 1732 onwards, Moravian missionaries were sent to the Islands of St. Thomas, the Virgin Islands, Greenland, North America, Lapland, South America, South Africa, Labrador, Australia and to the Tibetan border. The ratio of their full-time missionaries to those who stayed at home praying was a remarkable 1 to 60. That was 1.66% of their community, compared to 0.1% of UK evangelicals going overseas as missionaries today (according to *Operation World*).

> *It is time to recapture the heart-pounding awareness of the nearness and supernatural reality of God Himself walking with men in day to day life.*

This church of Bohemian Brethren became the Renewed Moravian Church. It was two of their Moravian missionaries, August Spangenburg and Peter Bohlers, who confronted John Wesley: 'Do you know yourself? Have you the witness within yourself? Does the Spirit of God bear witness with your spirit that you are a child of God?'

On 24 May 1738 Wesley describes his conversion: 'I felt my heart strangely warmed, I did trust in Christ alone for salvation. I was given assurance of my salvation and that He had taken away my sins, and saved me from the law of sin and death.'

The Moravians emphasized a life-centred faith believing in a God for whom nothing is impossible. Much has been written about their exploits, and these powerful and thought-provoking verses reflect their testimony. For many years they have been written in the front of my Bible:

- *The iron did swim* (2 Kings 6:6)
- *The sun stood still* (Joshua 10:13)
- THIS IS OUR GOD!

This constantly reminds me of how almighty and unchanging is the God we serve. He encourages us not to fear, nor be dismayed, because He will strengthen, help and uphold us with His righteous right hand (Isaiah 41:10).

First steps on the road

For my part, the journey began when I was in my twenties. I had dreamed of a professional career in football but sadly didn't quite make the grade. I began studying accountancy and qualified as a management accountant.

My spiritual journey began at Gold Hill Baptist Church in Gerrards Cross through the anointed ministry of Rev. Jim Graham. I knew immediately that God wanted me to be involved in worldwide mission. My parents, brothers and sister were all very supportive. With amazement, and yet godly wisdom, Jim and the elders gave their blessing and I, as a new Christian, embarked almost immediately on two years' missionary training in Glasgow. This was followed by a one-year assistant pastoral role at Trinity Baptist Church, Chesham.

I went to Thailand in 1978 with the aim of planting churches with WEC International. There I met Wilma, a missionary from Holland, who had been living in Thailand since 1972. We married in Kamphaeng Phet, north-west Thailand in 1981. We shared our calling and passion for planting churches, and our three children, Paul, Esther and Karen, were very much part of this early adventure, helping us to build relationships and understanding in the Thai community.

As I look back, it is immensely fulfilling to have seen Thai people come to faith, churches come into being, and the very unassuming become significant players for God in the development and growth of His Church.

Our ministry gradually widened, co-planting a church in Bangkok which is now influential in many parts of the nation. Invitations came to speak in Singapore and Malaysia, and then involvement in a rural church planting organisation in Sri Lanka opened up in 1994. It was whilst in Colombo that Dr. Dieter Kuhl, then international director for WEC, invited us to consider becoming regional directors for South East Asia. We believed that God had been preparing us for this role. We joyfully carried out the overseeing of mission teams in nine countries, focussing on church planting, for a total of 13 years.

Today, there is no greater joy for Wilma and myself than to encourage missionaries in their task of world evangelisation and church planting. Preaching and teaching at conferences fires something within us, and our current involvement with WEC Betel in a leadership training capacity gives us identity, commitment and accountability.

What about this new road?

I have shared a very brief overview of our ministry road with a specific purpose in mind. We can look back, whether a few years or many, and reflect on the testimony of God's faithfulness. To remember is a scriptural command as God for His part remembers His promises and His people.

Remembering helps us to worship. It inspires us with hope for tomorrow, infuses us with fresh courage and strength and also leads us to repentance, as we will discover later on in this book. At the same time the Holy Spirit causes us to face a reality check, comparing what we have heard and understood with what we have experienced and are currently living out.

Looking back and remembering is critical to looking forward. Remember the times God refused to let go when we had almost given up! Remember His understanding, love, care and provision that left us feeling humbled that He should oversee our lives with such detail! Remember the days when men had all but given up on us, and the voice of God came to us saying, *'I will never leave you nor forsake you'* (Hebrews 13:5 NKJV)! Remember the many occasions when we were anything but fruitful in ministry, and really wondered why bother to continue! Then our compassionate God spoke: *'I will restore to you the years that the . . . locust has eaten'* (Joel 2:25 NKJV).

Remembering must not leave us just looking back, but must be the means of moving us forward. It has the potential to take us out of the dead-end road of self-satisfaction, contentment and complacency. It can make us lift our head and see afresh into the heart of God who longs to open our eyes to the new road and journey ahead.

How can we be self-satisfied, especially in the light of 1 Corinthians 2:9: *'No eye has seen, no ear has heard, no mind has conceived what God has prepared for those who love Him'*?

Our understanding is so limited, even that of the wisest, but the Holy Spirit desires to take us into a new realm of understanding and experience. God is still our Amazing God.

When I realise that today we are still living in Bangkok, travelling across Asia and Europe, Wilma after 43 years on the mission field, and I 37 years on the mission field, this leaves me truly amazed at the miracle of His grace. And yet, despite the temptation to slow down, I find myself being challenged today by the Spirit of God to genuinely evaluate the present in order to move into the next level of God's purpose and plan.

Caleb had a different spirit (Numbers 14:24), and despite his advancing years he had no intention of settling into a convenient routine of spiritual life. What inspires me is his courage and faith in the mountain-moving ability of God, to go up and take the land (Numbers 13:30).

Mixed feelings!
This generates an excitement at the thought of moving forward with God and seeing His Kingdom come. At the same time there is a measure of hesitation and uneasiness, not only in facing an ever-increasing opposition to Christianity (like the giants of Anak in Numbers 13:32), but in knowing the degree of personal challenge and change that God will require in me.

CHAPTER 3

The need for a new encounter with God

Now Moses was tending the flock of Jethro his father-in-law, the priest of Midian, and he led the flock to the far side of the desert and came to Horeb, the mountain of God. There the angel of the LORD appeared to him in flames of fire from within a bush. Moses saw that though the bush was on fire it did not burn up. So Moses thought, 'I will go over and see this strange sight – why the bush does not burn up.'

When the LORD saw that he had gone over to look, God called to him from within the bush, 'Moses! Moses!' And Moses said, 'Here I am.'

'Do not come any closer,' God said. 'Take off your sandals, for the place where you are standing is holy ground.' Then He said, 'I am the God of your father, the God of Abraham, the God of Isaac and the God of Jacob.' At this, Moses hid his face, because he was afraid to look at God. (Exodus 3:1–6)

The life of Moses to me is a wonderful blend of challenge, encouragement and inspiration. What is the connection between Exodus 33 and Exodus 3?

Moses' situation in Exodus 33 mirrors what I perceive to be a personal and church/mission challenge now. It is currently a very popular section of Scripture and much

11

is being shared about Moses and the presence and glory of the Lord, and rightly so. In all our enthusiasm we may be tempted to immediately pick up our tents and move ahead. *But are we ready for that move?*

Certainly Exodus 33 is crucial in the life of Moses and the future journey of God's people. Which way will they go? To what degree will they allow God to be totally God in their lives? Will they really go out and out for God or will they be tempted and lured into a convenient, popular and respectable alternative which may gain admiration from many but not necessarily from God Himself?

Perhaps the well-used phrase '*to go forward we need to go back*' comes into play at this point.

Moses had been on quite a journey. Let's retrace his steps back to Exodus 3 and the burning bush and the passage at the beginning of this chapter. Why? Because the ways of God have a pattern and design to them and no matter what stage of God's journey we may be on, these basics steps often need to be remembered, heeded and repeated. Exodus chapter 3 is about a *supernatural moment* with God.

> *The angel of the LORD appeared to him in flames of fire from within a bush. . . . God called to him from within the bush, 'Moses! Moses!' And Moses said, 'Here I am.' . . . God said, 'Take off your sandals, for the place where you are standing is holy ground.'*

In the Old Testament, God took on various visible forms to show Himself to people, and manifest His presence and glory. These appearances of God are referred to as theophanies. The content of theophanies is basically the same. They consistently show God graciously revealing

Himself and His Presence and Glory to His people. In the burning bush the holiness of God was revealed (Exodus 3:5) – a frightening encounter, but one in which God also showed great compassion in allowing Moses to meet Him in this personal way.

Personal encounters in the New Testament supremely focus on Jesus, the radiance of the Father's glory (Hebrews 1:3). The Holy Spirit makes it His primary ministry to reveal to us that Jesus is both Lord and Christ (Acts 2:36).

Saul on the Damascus road experienced this encounter, meeting with the risen Christ in Acts 9:3–6:

As he (Saul) neared Damascus on his journey, suddenly a light from heaven flashed around him. He fell to the ground and heard a voice say to him, 'Saul, Saul why do you persecute me?' 'Who are you, Lord?' Saul asked. 'I am Jesus, whom you are persecuting,' he replied. 'Now get up and go into the city, and you will be told what you must do.'

Supernatural moments of man meeting with God in varied and remarkable ways run consistently through Scripture. Returning to the Old Testament we see that Joshua, Moses' young assistant, was to experience a theophany prior to the challenge of Jericho in Joshua 5:13–15.

Now when Joshua was near Jericho, he looked up and saw a man standing in front of him with a drawn sword in his hand. Joshua went up to him and asked, 'Are you for us or for our enemies?' 'Neither,' he replied, 'but as commander of the army of the LORD I have now come.' Then Joshua fell face down to the ground in reverence, and asked him, 'What message does my Lord have for his servant?' The commander of the LORD's army replied, 'Take off your sandals, for the place where you are standing is holy.' And Joshua did so.

Whether it be Moses, Joshua, Isaiah, Saul (Paul) or ourselves, surely it can be no other way. We too need a new encounter with God. Why? Because we seldom realise what it means to move upwards and onwards in the purpose and plan of God. Even in our best spiritual moments we are so woefully unaware of His majesty and holiness.

Isaiah, having had such an experience, later writes: *'For my thoughts are not your thoughts, neither are your ways my ways,'* declares the LORD. *'As the heavens are higher than the earth, so are my ways higher than your ways and my thoughts than your thoughts'* (Isaiah 55:8–9).

How else will God get our attention other than by a supernatural moment? Often the spiritual ministry and serving track we are on can just carry on automatically; remember the jumbo jet being unable to land!

This activity is often driven by familiarity (I have always done things like this), personal preference (this is what I want or like to do), and sometimes by human pressure (this is what is expected of me), rather than by anointing and presence.

Exodus 33 is a crossroad point in Moses' leadership and the people's movement towards the Promised Land. The backward reflection to Exodus 3 reminds Moses, and us, that *you do not drift casually* into the purposes, calling and future plans of God. Down through the centuries God has reinforced this truth in the lives of so many.

D. L. Moody, an example

The year 1871 was a critical one in Mr Moody's career. He realised more and more how inadequate he was for the enormous challenge of the work ahead of him. An intense hunger and thirst for spiritual power were aroused in him by two women who used to attend the meetings and sit on the front seat. He could see by the expression on their faces that they were praying. At the close of services they would say to him, 'We have been praying for you.' 'Why don't you pray for the people?' Mr. Moody would ask. 'Because you need the power of the Spirit,' they would say. 'I need the power! Why,' said Mr. Moody, relating the incident years after, 'I thought I had power. I had the largest congregations in Chicago, and there were many conversions. I was in a sense satisfied. But right along those two godly women kept praying for me, and their earnest talk about anointing for special service set me thinking. I asked them to come and talk with me, and they poured out their hearts in prayer that I might receive the anointing of the Holy Spirit. There came a great hunger into my soul. I did not know what it was. I began to cry out as I never did before. I really felt that I did not want to live if I could not have this power for service.'

As I spent time thinking about Moses, Joshua, Isaiah, Saul (Paul), D. L. Moody and now my own situation, I too began to be aware of the need for personal revival once again, without which the challenge of future ministry appeared all too daunting.

Two reasons became immediately clear to me (I'm sure there are many more) as to why a supernatural moment with God is crucial to the next stage of the journey:

1. Because no matter how gifted we are that is never enough!

Moses was very gifted; Acts 7:22 tells us he was 'educated in all the wisdom of the Egyptians and was powerful in speech and action'. However, when we approach either the starting point of God's mission or subsequent challenges to move onwards and upwards, it is not unusual in that supernatural godly moment to end up feeling absolutely useless and incapable of fulfilling that calling.

Moses had an advantage over us. The last 40 years had removed nearly every trace of superiority, self-confidence and self-sufficiency. He believed, as a murderer on the run, that he was the last person God could and would use.

> The LORD said, 'I have indeed seen the misery of my people in Egypt. I have heard them crying out because of their slave drivers, and I am concerned about their suffering. So I have come down to rescue them from the hand of the Egyptians and to bring them up out of that land into a good and spacious land, a land flowing with milk and honey – the home of the Canaanites, Hittites, Amorites, Perizzites, Hivites and Jebusites. And now the cry of the Israelites has reached me, and I have seen the way the Egyptians are oppressing them. So now, go. I am sending you to Pharaoh to bring my people the Israelites out of Egypt.' (Exodus 3:7–10)

Moses' response to God's commission to 'send him to Pharaoh' shows us his view of himself:

- he was insignificant – 'who am I' (Exodus 3:11);
- he was ignorant – 'I have nothing to say' (Exodus 3:13);
- he was impotent – 'they will never listen to me' (Exodus 4:1);
- he was incompetent – 'I can't put two words together without stammering' (Exodus 4:10);
- he was irrelevant – 'please send someone else' (Exodus 4:13).

In the privileged years of overseeing missionaries, we have met so many capable and gifted people, who in the eyes of the world (and the church) should be prime candidates for fruitful, ground-breaking ministry . . . but somehow that did not happen.

For many years I could count myself as one of them. The calling was there, the training was there, the preparation seemed complete. But what about the encounter?

Whilst Moses was probably feeling like a washed-out rag, a waste of space, irrelevant to God and of little use to anyone, God's life-transforming, supernatural moment was about to happen in his life.

In the New Testament Paul says he had every reason to be confident in the flesh. He had a pedigree spiritual upbringing (Philippians 3:4–6):

- circumcised on the eighth day
- an Israelite, coming from the tribe of Benjamin
- a Hebrew of Hebrews
- in regard to the law a Pharisee
- as for zeal, persecuting the church
- as for legalistic righteousness, faultless.

And yet that encounter on the Damascus road in Acts 9 began a massive transformation. In order for us to understand more clearly what this transformation is like, Paul uses a Greek word *metamorphoo* in 2 Corinthians 3:18:

And we, who with unveiled faces all reflect the Lord's glory, are being transformed into his likeness with ever-increasing glory, which comes from the Lord, who is the Spirit.

There are two important things to consider at this point.

17

First, the Spirit always moves us to Christ. He does not do His own thing or work to another agenda. The Holy Spirit generates experience, and then in that experience moves us to Christ. This is the centre of His ministry to bring men and women to confess that *'Jesus is Lord'* (1 Corinthians 12:3).

Secondly, Paul is pointing out to us that being 'changed from one degree of glory to another' (RSV) is not a minor event passing with little effect and change. These moments and encounters are massive times of transformation, indeed, as significant as a caterpillar changing into a butterfly (metamorphosis).

Therefore the ministry of the Spirit changes the form and shape of who we are, renewing us and re-charging us with divine glory that transforms us more and more into the likeness of Jesus.

Paul continues that his change is not a once in a life-time experience, but in 2 Corinthians 3:18 'change' is in the present continuous tense. There can be no sense of thinking that we have arrived, but an increasing aware-ness of how much more change needs to take place, in a ceaseless, dynamic, progressive way.

A crucial truth to understand at this point is that this is something **done in us** and not something **we do**! We open ourselves in faith; even this is not us but the work of the Holy Spirit. Paul is also not just thinking of a personal experience, significant though that is, but a corporate experience as the Body of Christ. It is the church as God's people reflecting this glory as seen in Acts 2, manifesting the things that Christ *'has poured out what you now see and hear'* (Acts 2:33).

The fellowship of the Church together encounter these on-going life-changing moments in the Spirit . . . with the one supreme goal to make us more like Jesus. So Paul's encounter on the Damascus road and his subsequent encounters bring about a massive ministry change which takes him from being confident in the flesh in Philippians 3:4–6 to 1 Corinthians 2:4–5:

> My message and my preaching were not with wise and persuasive words, but with a demonstration of the Spirit's power, so that your faith might not rest on men's wisdom, but on God's power.

The change is like night and day.

Supernatural moments challenge men's wisdom and their motives. This has to be because God's ways and our ways are so far apart. The wisdom of men is destructive because it uses the human mind to find an alternative to God's purpose, plan and way of salvation. Why? Simply because human wisdom loves to boast before God and man (1 Corinthians 1:29).

Throughout history, it has not been theological arguments and gifted oratory that have moved men and women for God. It has been revelation and encounter. How many times I must have grieved the Spirit of God by trying to be clever in ministry. The bush was burning with the glory of God. Moses was given a revelation of God and His purposes for Israel. This was to shape him as a leader, and also the people.

Early days in Thailand
In my early years in Thailand I used to ride my Honda motorbike to small, scattered village church home groups

in the north-west, encouraging and teaching them from the Word of God. I remember returning home feeling very proud of myself. The village farmers had actually understood what I was sharing and they seemed to enjoy my visit. Then suddenly, God spoke, not in an audible voice, but in an unmistakeable way nonetheless. 'Mike, why did you share that passage of Scripture?' Well, I tried to provide a good answer to God but really struggled. I liked that passage of Scripture. It has spoken to me many times. I enjoyed speaking about it, and the people seem to like it too. But I knew in my heart these were just excuses; I could not honestly say that the Spirit of God had shown me clearly that this portion of Scripture was what they needed to hear that day.

Furthermore, I felt even more uncomfortable when God said, 'Mike, by the way, why are you feeling proud of yourself?'

I had to confess it was because I was pleased with my Thai language, kind of proud that I had managed to bridge the gap between West and East. Whilst that in itself is not necessarily wrong, God didn't let me off the hook and said, 'While you are returning home feeling pleased with yourself, having had a good meeting, do you realise that the unsaved are still unsaved, that the sick are still ill, that the oppressed are still in bondage? When will you let me have *my* meeting?'

Whilst the worldly wisdom Paul mentions in Corinthians is wisdom opposed to the ways of God, I realised that there is also a worldly wisdom which looks amazingly spiritual and godly but seeks to do God's work our way. However gifted we may be, when used inappropriately the gifts can get in the way of God's will and purpose. A supernatural visitation from God forces us to come to Him with open and empty hands.

Toplady wrote the hymn *Rock of Ages* in 1763 and some lines just fit at this point.

Nothing in my hand I bring,
Simply to Thy cross I cling;
Naked, come to Thee for dress;
Helpless, look to Thee for grace . . .

Without realising it, the way Moses saw the last 40 years of his life was about to change dramatically. The pride, self-confidence and self-belief were no longer there. He had disqualified himself from being a candidate for God's mission.

The educated orator filled with the wisdom of the world, this strong man with so much leadership potential and gifting was now looking like the least likely person to rescue God's people and lead them into the Promised Land.

It seems to me that this is the place to which God wants to bring us. It is not about you and me with our gifting and ability. Supremely it is about being clay in the Potter's hand.

For Moses and for us, despite our gifting and ability, there are times when we find ourselves in the wilderness of hopelessness, frustration and even fruitlessness. It is here that we struggle and discover that '*the foolishness of God is wiser than man's wisdom, and the weakness of God is stronger than man's strength*' (1 Corinthians 1:25).

Whilst the worldly wisdom Paul mentions in Corinthians is wisdom opposed to the ways of God, I realised that there is also a worldly wisdom which looks amazingly spiritual and godly but seeks to do God's work our way.

---

2. Because God needs to catch our attention.

A supernatural moment with God not only takes our eyes off what we think we can do for God, through our gifts and abilities, but is also God's sovereign way of catching our attention. Our eyes are opened anew to see that we cannot drift casually into the purposes, calling and future plans of God, no matter how able and capable we think we may be.

For Moses it was a burning bush; not so remarkable in a desert, except that the bush was on fire but not burning. Whatever it may be for you and me, it will most probably be something that has the same effect as it had on Moses, turning mild interest into 'godly fear'.

The last three years have been in many respects life-transforming and humbling for me. God has been turning my attention to revival. Not just to pray, prepare and long for revival, but more to discover the life-changing impact the Holy Spirit had on people's lives when His power was released. It continues to be a sobering exercise.

Let me give you just one example.

On Monday, 7 November 2011, I had a dream which I initially thought was neither helpful nor instructive. I clearly heard the words 'Go downstairs'. I went downstairs and found that I had left the patio doors wide open all night. All the valuable items had been stolen.

So real was the dream that I woke up in a cold sweat. As I reflected on this I just knew that the Spirit was challenging me to walk carefully and to change my ways. It was as if God was saying to me, 'Mike, if my presence goes with you and if I show you my glory, you can't carry on living carelessly where the treasures of heaven can be so easily stolen.' The mild interest I had walking down the stairs turned into 'godly fear'.

In Exodus 33 God was causing Moses and the people to focus on the land of Canaan ahead. However, learning from the past is necessary in order to move forward into God's present. For Moses it all began with a supernatural moment in Exodus 3, and to move forward now in Exodus 33 would require no less. If we were Moses we may have said: 'Lord, I thought the experience I had 30 chapters ago would be enough for the rest of my life?!'

In Chapter Eight I will take the following thoughts a little further.

- There are measures of faith: no faith, little faith and great faith. In the same way I know there are measures of glory, and we are being changed from one degree of glory to another (2 Corinthians 3:18).
- In the context of the Kingdom of God coming, and the Father longing to give us the Holy Spirit, the exhortation is to *'ask and keep on asking, seek and keep on seeking, knock and keep on knocking'* (Luke 11:9 Amplified). Why? Because there is always more of the Holy Spirit to receive.
- The Father loves to increase the manifestation of His love, joy, peace and power to His children (Luke 11:9–13). D. L. Moody adds another reason: when asked why he was seeking more of the Holy Spirit, he replied, 'Because I leak!'

My personal mission journey over these years has been a huge learning curve. The greater part of this has had less to do with powerful ministry and more to do with learning how to walk ever closer with God.

Many years ago, God challenged me over who my hero was. I could mention all the great prophets – especially the apostle Paul and his church planting and mission exploits. But then God turned my attention to a person who I had honestly overlooked completely. Someone who had never planted a church or been known for great mission adventure; his name was Enoch. The reason became so clear when I read what Enoch was famous and known for. . . . *he walked with God!*

How often I have had to *look back* and learn afresh that the next phase of ministry has more to do with 'encountering God' than 'ministry for God'. I can personally recall seven occasions which for me were 'supernatural moments', not a great track record when it spans a period of nearly 40 years! What about you?

On each of these occasions God had a different reason for getting my attention. For example, at the time when the church planting work in Thailand was becoming fruitful and blessed, with people coming to faith and small groups being established, I had another dream and encounter.

I had a big filing box which I presented to God. It contained all the sermons I had preached, the places where I had gone to share the gospel, the churches and leaders' meetings that I had attended and spoken at, and the prayer letters I had written to my home church.

I was pleased to present this trophy to God. As I handed it to Him, He didn't seem too interested or pleased. The smile began to fall from my face too. Then He spoke: 'Mike, put the box down and stretch out your arm.' I did so, and the Lord put two fingers on my pulse. He then spoke: 'All this effort, work and ministry, and I can hardly find the pulse beat of love for Me.' I was shattered, but then I needed to be. The words of Revelation 2:2–5 came powerfully to me:

I know your deeds, your hard work and your perseverance. I know that you cannot tolerate wicked men, that you have tested those who claim to be apostles but are not, and have found them false. You have

persevered and have endured hardships for my name,
and have not grown weary.
Yet I hold this against you:

You have forsaken your first love. *Remember the height*
from which you have fallen! Repent and do the things
you did at first.

There is so much more to God than I currently know and
have experienced. How proud to think that I do not need
another encounter with this Majestic and All-powerful
God!

An encounter, to me, is receiving first a fresh vision of
God Himself, then an awareness of the foolishness of our
wisdom, and a willingness to translate that foolishness
into being a 'fool' for God.

Reflection point

God is challenging us to go on His journey. This will be
like travelling on an unfamiliar road, and will require us
to recognise and allow God to do something new in our
lives. Yes, a new encounter that bathes our gifting in the
fresh Presence of God and enables Him to catch our attention concerning the coming journey.

CHAPTER 4

'Take off your ornaments'

> *Throughout history it has not been theological arguments and gifted oratory that have moved men and women for God. It has been revelation and encounter.*

For the LORD had said to Moses, 'Tell the Israelites, "You are a stiff-necked people. If I were to go with you even for a moment, I might destroy you. Now take off your ornaments and I will decide what to do with you." ' So the Israelites stripped off their ornaments at Mount Horeb. (Exodus 33:5–6)

From Exodus chapter 3 to chapter 33 we see a godly man leading a not so godly people with astonishing dedication and perseverance. During this time Moses had witnessed some remarkable miracles. Turning bitter water into sweet drinking water; the provision of manna and quails; water from a rock – they hadn't lacked anything! And then what about the dramatic victories over many enemies much stronger and better equipped than them (Deuteronomy 2)?

God had given Moses the privilege of seeing His signs and wonders on an almost daily basis. Even more than this, he had the promises of God ringing in his ears:

- *I will free you* (Exodus 6:6)
- *I will redeem you* (Exodus 6:6)
- *I will make you my own people* (Exodus 6:7)
- *I will give you Canaan, a land flowing with milk and honey* (Exodus 6:8)
- *I will drive out all the enemies* (Exodus 6:8)

For a missionary to witness these promises makes any sacrifice and hardship seem insignificant. This is what we live for and, if necessary, die for. Whilst mission today can involve a very broad and all-embracing ministry, it is the power of the gospel alone that will bring people out of the slave market of sin to be reconciled to the Father through His Son Jesus Christ.

The need for anointed evangelists must still be the biggest single need in missions today. I know of so many genuine and godly men and women serving in many parts of Asia and doing a fantastic job. However, I have heard few who, with tears in their eyes and a heart burdened for the lost, are crying out to God for a new anointing of the Spirit to preach and demonstrate the gospel in the power of the Spirit.

Certainly within the WEC Betel world over the last 27 years God has done some great things. The testimonies of freedom have inspired and challenged us. The testimonies of His provision on a daily basis have amazed us. The testimonies of His redeeming love birthing leaders of great maturity have left us speechless. The testimonies of the defeat of enemies wishing to derail Betel and its ministry have brought worship to a high level. The testimonies of His vision opening up eyes to see His future have given a desire to live and breathe Matthew 28:18–20 and Acts 1:8.

Yes, of course there have been fleshly struggles, as Moses and the people witnessed in the desert. Yes, there have been times of division, disagreement and dissatisfaction, but God has been compassionate and gracious, slow to anger and abounding in love, faithfulness, grace and mercy – a word that He was going to remind them of in Exodus 34:6–7.

But first, we need to look at Exodus 32:

When the people saw that Moses was so long in coming down from the mountain, they gathered round Aaron and said, 'Come, make us gods who will go before us. As for this fellow Moses who brought us up out of Egypt, we don't know what has happened to him.'

Aaron answered them, 'Take off the gold ear-rings that your wives, your sons and your daughters are wearing, and bring them to me.' So all the people took off their ear-rings and brought them to Aaron. He took what they handed him and made it into an idol cast in the shape of a calf, fashioning it with a tool. Then they said, 'These are your gods, O Israel, who brought you up out of Egypt . . .'

Then the LORD said to Moses, 'Go down, because your people, whom you brought up out of Egypt, have become corrupt. They have been quick to turn away from what I commanded them and have made themselves an idol cast in the shape of a calf. They have bowed down to it and sacrificed to it and have said, "These are your gods, O Israel, who brought you up out of Egypt."

'I have seen these people,' the LORD said to Moses, 'and they are a stiff-necked people. Now leave me alone so that my anger may burn against them and that I may destroy them. Then I will make you into a great nation.'

But Moses sought the favour of the LORD his God. 'O LORD,' he said, 'why should your anger burn against your people, whom you brought out of Egypt with great power and a mighty hand? . . . 'Remember your servants Abraham, Isaac and Israel, to whom you swore by your own self: "I will make your descendants as numerous as the stars in the sky and I will give your descendants all this land I promised them, and it will be their inheritance for ever." ' Then the LORD relented and did not bring on his people the disaster he had threatened.

Reading these verses makes it more clear to me that we can't look at Exodus 33 without mentioning Exodus 32! It brings home clearly to my own heart (like in that dream of the patio doors) that despite all the miracles and blessings we have received, it doesn't take much for the old life to reappear. Despite who we may think we are, what we have achieved and witnessed, and what position we may now hold, we are not as spiritual as we like to think. We might not resort to physically making a 'golden calf', but the spiritual equivalents appear all too easily in our lives. They often spring from 'look what *we* have made with our own hand' or 'look what has been produced, designed, and shaped by *us*'.

Isn't this the constant challenge to those of us who have opportunities to preach, teach and minister in a variety of situations, and particularly so if we have a visible 'up-front' ministry?

Maybe it begins with the temptation to preach out of human wisdom rather than what God is processing in and through us, the message of truth becoming detached from our own lives. How different is that to the Apostle Paul in Romans 15:17–18: *'Therefore I glory in Christ Jesus in my service to God. I will not venture to speak of anything except what Christ has accomplished through me in leading the Gentiles to obey God by what I have said and done.'*

Another handle that seeks to open the door of pride is to create an image of maturity and wisdom when the truth is anything but this – to give the impression of success and fruitfulness because after 40 years in ministry people expect that. How tempting to embellish the newsletters we write home! How tempting to use the energy and initiative of the flesh to shine our work for God and make it look so much more successful than it really is!

Early Bangkok experience

In the early days of planting the church in Bangkok, we met in the Alexandra Hotel. The neutral venue was important because a hotel made it easier for Thai non-Christians to come and go without undue pressure. The church was beginning to grow. People, mostly young people and students, were coming to Christ on a regular basis. The worship was uplifting and I have to say loud, but the Holy Spirit was working in a significant and encouraging way. We had seen some miraculous healings and there was a real buzz of expectancy as we met every Sunday.

After one Sunday morning meeting I saw someone talking with Aajarn [Thai for *teacher*] Sangwian, who was co-leading the church plant. I had not seen that person before, and when I asked what the conversation was about, he explained the matter to me. That person was

30

a missionary sent by their local church. Their intention was to plant a church, and a building had been rented with accommodation. A big sign was placed outside the building naming the church. Pictures of this had been taken and sent back to the supporting church. There was only one problem: there were no believers. Under pressure from the home church to 'be successful', and desperate to send back pictures showing this, that missionary came this morning with an open cheque book to buy our church.

That may seem extreme, and our immediate reaction no doubt is to be hyper-critical and amazed that someone would go to such lengths, but on reflection I came to realise that, in differing degrees, it is a fleshly battle we all have – namely, to appear to be more spiritual and fruitful than is really the case.

Whatever our 'golden calves' may be, one thing is certain: that we all struggle with them, varied as they are in both shape and design. There may also be some truth in the claim that the more successful we are, the greater opportunity the golden calves have to grow in size and number.

Note the precise timing of these calves! All of this comes just when God desires to move us into the next stage of our journey with Him. Not only do old golden calves come back to haunt and taunt us, but new ones are presented. Whether old or new they have one intention: to corrupt us and derail us from God's purpose and plan for our lives.

Calf worship symbolised fertility and strength. It is amazing the lengths that the flesh will go to in order to appear fruitful and strong and gain the praise, admiration and even continuing support that is required to keep the ministry going. The heart of the issue may simply be in preferring and desiring to have something visible to follow rather than walking by faith.

An old Pentecostal missionary, a man of unshakeable faith in the Word of God, was heard to say, 'Brethren, the Spirit of God is with us still. Pentecost is yet within our grasp. If revival is being withheld from us it is because some idols remain still enthroned; because we still insist in placing our reliance in human schemes; because we still refuse to face the unchangeable truth that it is "not by might nor by power but by my Spirit".' How true!

A key question at this point is: what kick-started all this calf worship in the first place?

Israel may have become corrupt, but their religious life continued, and they still sacrificed burnt offerings and presented fellowship offerings. The heart of the matter was *impatience,* which seems so ordinary. After all, Moses took so long to come down from the mountain (Exodus 32:1).

Whilst impatience has been described as a strong sense of annoyance or exasperation, it has a twin called irritability. This describes the frequency of impatience. Together, impatience and irritability, though appearing so ordinary and acceptable, are in fact lethal weapons of spiritual destruction.

The lessons of the past come back to us. Abraham and Sarah did not wait for God to give them a son. Esau's impatience cost him his birthright. Saul was impatient waiting for Samuel, and moved into a ministry not ordained of God, from which he never recovered.

In the New Testament, one of the crucial apostolic characteristics was patience (2 Corinthians 12:12 RSV). The Greek word *hupomone* carries the meaning of patience and endurance. It is used in connection with hope (Romans 5:3), faith (James 1:3) and joy (Colossians 1:11). It is this patience which radiantly hopes for the dawn of a new day, knowing only God can bring that day into being. It is not for man to manufacture or try to create, but it is totally dependent on waiting for and being obedient to the leading and timing of the Spirit of God.

The 'golden thread' of truth woven at the time of Moses was to be continued (Exodus 40:36–38). Whenever the cloud lifted the people moved out. If it stood still, so did they. The same applied to the fire by night. From the time of Moses, through the Old Testament and into the New Testament, the importance of patience and waiting on God is paramount. The principle of Exodus 40:36–38, that whenever the cloud by day or the fire at night lifted, it is time to move, seems so obvious and simple, and yet in practice, patience and waiting on God is so hard.

In their encounter with the Holy Spirit in Acts 2, this vital lesson was also being etched onto the heart of the newly birthed church. Unless the Spirit of God moved, they stood still. It was the principle that Jesus Himself had so clearly shared with His disciples: *'By myself I can do nothing; I judge only as I hear, and my judgement is just, for I seek not to please myself but him who sent me'* (John 5:30).

Jesus' effectiveness in ministry was not from 'dazzling divinity' but anointed humanity. This is a picture of what He can do in us, preparing, changing and shaping us into mature manhood, yes, even to the measure of the stature of the fullness of Christ.

Jesus is both the bearer of the Holy Spirit, receiving it at His baptism (John 1:33), and the giver of the Holy Spirit for mission. Doctor Luke makes sure we understand this:

John answered them all, 'I baptise you with water. But one more powerful than I will come, the thongs of whose sandals I am not worthy to untie. He will baptise you with the Holy Spirit and with fire.' (Luke 3:16) Exalted to

the right hand of God, he (Jesus) has received from the
Father the promised Holy Spirit and has poured out what
you now see and hear. (Acts 2:33)

Why else would Jesus say in John 16:7 (RSV), 'it is to your advantage that I go away'? For the task of evangelising the world, building His church and expanding His Kingdom, the immediate presence of the Third Person of the Trinity would be more important to them than the immediate presence of the Second and, as we know, the book of Acts is about the acts of the Holy Spirit.

The amazing truth is that this is the same Holy Spirit that empowered and equipped Jesus for life and ministry (Luke 3:21–22, 4:1, 4:18–19); enabled Jesus to heal the sick, deliver the demonic, release the oppressed, and preach the Gospel in power to the poor; enabled Jesus to do signs and wonders; raised Jesus from the dead (Romans 8:11); and *is to come upon us* (Acts 1:8), so that we 'do' and 'teach' in the same way Jesus did (Acts 1:1). Again Jesus said, *'Peace be with you! As the Father has sent me, I am sending you'* (John 20:21).

As I mentioned earlier, with 25–27% of the world still waiting to hear the Gospel and so many opportunities for ministry, the importance of totally depending upon the Spirit of God screams at us through the chapters of Acts.

It seems to me that this is the principal reason why, in just 30 years, the Gospel succeeded in spreading from Jerusalem to Rome. All appears so simple and straight-forward, and yet the flesh favours impatience and 'my way' over God's way. How many of our current strategies, visions and programmes are founded from a patient, per-severing heart that refuses to move unless that move is initiated by the leading of the Spirit of God?

Apostolic anointing birthed spiritual authority, a hunger for the truth of God's Word, signs, wonders and healing and much more. But the centre of this was a heart of submission to God. Patience is waiting for God, and impatience is running ahead of God. How many times have we heard the words of A. W. Tozer that if the Spirit of God was withdrawn, the majority of work in the church would continue as normal? How relevant is Tozer's challenge to us? Has work *for God* taken priority over working *with God*?

Can you and I identify recurring situations in our lives that tempt us to become impatient? This question is not asking whether we have a problem with impatience, but are we ever impatient? For so long I had not grasped the seriousness of letting impatience roam freely in my life. How often have I condemned the more obvious sins of society and tolerated impatience and irritability?

The difficulty with the challenge of impatience is that it is so familiar to all of us that we consider it normal rather than a sin. Exodus 32 brings the seriousness of impatience to the forefront of our attention. The next level of God's calling and journey must cause us to see the potential destruction that impatience can bring to our spiritual lives and address this issue seriously.

I have always loved reading about the great Chinese revival and the ministry of Dr. Jonathan Goforth in 1908. In Chihli deep conviction fell upon the people, falling to their knees as they prayed (usually they stood). Within minutes, hundreds had fallen to their knees. Suddenly, like a wind sweeping over a field of grain, the Holy Spirit caused every man, woman and child to fall to the floor asking for mercy.

But it is *the key to the Chihli revival* that really grabbed my attention. The Holy Spirit had been working deeply in a renowned medical doctor, a brilliant man known far and wide for his piety. He admitted personally to impatience on one or two occasions over the last six months. When the doctor humbled himself in public confession, the Chihli revival came in full force. This story made a big impression on my life, especially 'one or two occasions over the last six months'!

Whilst this chapter has focused upon impatience and the corrupting influence it had in Exodus 32, it has also made me even more aware of God's hatred for sin. How fleshly to cover things over because they appear so normal and acceptable. When I read this account of the revival in Chihli I understood that many attitudes and thought patterns will need to drastically change for me, a church, or a mission organisation to move towards revival. Where? In me! In us!

CHAPTER 5

My way or your way?
The choice is yours

Another handle that seeks to open the door of pride is to create an image of maturity and wisdom when the truth is anything but this, to give the impression of success and fruitfulness.

Then the LORD said to Moses, 'Leave this place, you and the people you brought up out of Egypt, and go up to the land I promised on oath to Abraham, Isaac and Jacob, saying, "I will give it to your descendants." I will send an angel before you and will drive out the Canaanites, Amorites, Hittites, Perizzites, Hivites and Jebusites. Go up to the land flowing with milk and honey. But I will not go with you, because you are a stiff-necked people and I might destroy you on the way.'

When the people heard these distressing words, they began to mourn and no-one put on any ornaments. (Exodus 33:1–4)

The Lord speaks to Moses saying:

- leave this place, you and the people
- go up to the land I promised
- I will give the land to you

- I will send an angel to drive out the enemies
- the land will be as I said, flowing with milk and honey.

That seems wonderful; surely this is the moment they had all been waiting for. You can almost hear the buzz of excitement. After all, they have been dreaming of these promises and now God has spoken. But there's just one problem: 'I will not go with you.'

The buzz of excitement became silence and confusion, leaving them with a decision. What a challenge at this strategic time of opportunity and advance! What decision will be made? Where does their heart really lie? What are they all about?

You can have the land. You can be successful and victorious in ministry. You can achieve your vision, goals and financial objectives. You, your church and mission can grow, expand and be influential. Its impact can hit the front pages of the tabloids and mission journals. You can win the approval of organisations and missions, and be the central feature in the major Christian publications. All this and much more! For a mission agency it could mean multiple centres being established throughout the world. *God can send an angel to make you successful!*

How does this apply to you? Your personal ministry dream? The dream for your church or organisation? The goals you have prayed for regarding your nation and sphere of ministry? What if God should say, 'I will send an angel to fulfil all these dreams, but there is one thing you need to know: I will not be going with you.'

Two thoughts emerge from this:

1. **What would our response be?** I know what my initial response would be, but what would truthfully be the response from our heart? To say that this question may

be harder to answer than we first thought may appear strange to some. However, the combination of ministry expectation placed upon us and the struggle to be fruitful in an often hostile and unfriendly environment can tip the balance to desire success at any cost.

2. **Would we notice the difference** between an angel leading us and God Himself?

Let us look briefly at the real ministry of angels.

Angels have a servant role bathed in a lifestyle of worship (Luke 2:14). They deliver God's people from their enemies as in Acts 5:19 and 12:6–11, unlocking chains and opening prison doors. They also give guidance, revealing God's will, as with Philip in Acts 8:26. They bring hope in tough times, foretelling the birth of Jesus (Luke 2:9–12). They announced the resurrection of Jesus (Luke 24:4–7) and encouraged the faithful with the news of Jesus' Second Coming and final triumph (Acts 1:10–11).

Many people long to see angels in their lives and ministry as if that is the pinnacle of spiritual experience. But the writer to the Hebrews counsels that the focus of our attention ought not to be on angels, but on the Father's only son, Jesus. Jesus is the sovereign Lord and angels are His ministering servants. John in Revelation, on receiving his words of prophecy, was himself tempted to worship at the feet of an angel, but was redirected to worship God.

I, John, am the one who heard and saw these things. And when I had heard and seen them, I fell down to worship at the feet of the angel who had been showing them to me. But he said to me, 'Do not do it! I am a fellow-servant with you and with your brothers the prophets and of all who keep the words of this book. Worship God!' (Revelation 22:8–9)

God's test comes at strategic times of opportunity, as experienced by Jesus Himself in Matthew 4. The test for us is not so that we fall but that we come through as pure gold (Job 23:10). Our focus and dependence is on God alone.

Moses and the people could have experienced their hearts' desires as they entered Canaan, but God's presence and glory would not accompany them. This is the challenge: *is it success or God Himself?*

The danger with success and fruitful ministry is that we are tempted to be proud and say, 'Look what we have achieved with a little help from God.' Of course we would say this in a more subtle and spiritual way, but underneath I sense the spirit of Achan is very much alive and well, wanting to steal that which belongs to God alone.

> *Achan replied, 'It is true! I have sinned against the LORD, the God of Israel. This is what I have done: When I saw in the plunder a beautiful robe from Babylonia, two hundred shekels of silver and a wedge of gold weighing fifty shekels, I coveted them and took them. They are hidden in the ground inside my tent, with the silver underneath.'* (Joshua 7: 20–21)

Will He find a people who give Him *all* the spoil? Will He find a people who will give Him *all* the glory? Will He find a people who, like Paul, glory in their weakness so that the power of God may be seen?

How can we boast? How can we steal that which belongs to God? We did not rescue ourselves, raise ourselves up when dead in sin, deliver ourselves from fear, decide to follow and serve Jesus, cleanse ourselves from sin, change our lives, or empower ourselves for mission.

I wonder if this is not one of the biggest stumbling blocks and challenges facing us all. All the wonderful acts of provision and victory that had taken place in the desert were because God was in the midst of His people, nothing more and nothing less.

The serious question God seems to be asking at this point is, 'How important is my Presence to you?'

When we are struggling in difficult times, our need for God and His Presence is very evident. It results in us praying and crying out to God for a change of season from winter to spring, summer and harvest. Our barrenness in ministry brings us to our knees. But when the ministry is flowing, and fruit is evident, are we still on our knees crying out for His Presence to come in an ever-increasing, God-glorifying way? Or would we be satisfied, provided the blessing continues, with an angel leading us?

Paul's words of warning in Galatians 3:3 ring in our ears at this time of pressure to be user friendly, more acceptable to people, less fanatic, up-to-date and modern in mission approach. Though none of these are necessarily wrong in themselves, God's word still fires a warning shot across our desires and aspirations: *'Having begun with the Spirit are you now ending the flesh?'*(RSV)

In Jeremiah 6:16, Judah is close to celebrating 1000 years as a nation; 1000 years of progress, and yet God sent His prophet to speak out: *'Stand at the crossroads and look; ask for the ancient paths, ask where the good way is, and walk in it, and you will find rest for your souls.'*

Why walk the ancient ways and paths? Yesterday's world seems so primitive and basic, like comparing a typewriter with an iPad.

We have a choice at this point. Though our world today is vastly different from Exodus 33 and Jeremiah 6, the prophetic voice still speaks loud and clear. We need to stop, stand, consider and ask for the ancient paths and where the good way is, and then choose whether to walk in it or not.

WEC International Mission is 100 years old; Betel is 27 years old. The age is not the issue but each anniversary year, be it personal for us or as a church or mission, is an opportunity to recapture the spiritual dynamic that the Spirit of God was birthing in the beginning.

To the church-planting missionary, there are so many wonderful models of church life around the world. New approaches come thick and fast, and that is helpful to a degree, but it can also be both distracting and confusing. In the years of overseeing church-planting teams in Asia, questions related to church-planting methods have come one after another. This eager desire to be fruitful in ministry can also lead us into a frenzied round of importing every new idea that comes our way. This often leads into disappointment and a cul-de-sac experience. Why? Because what is appropriate and right in the West may well clash with what is appropriate and right in the East. The gospel is the power of God for every tribe, nation and culture; that is an unchallenged truth. But for that to be understood and received will require us to plug into the truth of Isaiah 55: 9 – *'my ways are higher than your ways'* – and will need the anointing of the Spirit and the gift of wisdom.

Every church-planter's heart must surely be rooted in Acts 2, when Jesus poured out the promised gift of the Holy Spirit. Yes, we need to look forward at the remaining challenges and take the gospel to the least and unreached, but modern ideas and the ideas of man today will never replace the spiritual dynamic that God was imparting to those 120 people in Acts 2.

As we finish this chapter Moses asks God an interesting question in Exodus 33:16: *'What . . . will distinguish me and your people from all the other people on the face of the earth?'*

Of course there will be a ministry distinctive, a strategic distinctive, a methodological distinctive, but that misses the point. The distinguishing feature of any relevant, vibrant and godly ministry will be the measure of the manifest Presence and Glory of God.

The glory of the Lord in this sense means the revealed person, character, work and power of the Lord Jesus Christ. In Christ, the glory of God becomes accessible and available to us. The power and glory belong to the Father, but are mediated in His Son Jesus, and then transferred to us by the Spirit.

God's challenge in Exodus 33 is about choice and whether or not His Presence will be our priority request and prayer. It highlights the struggle between what the New Testament calls 'flesh' and 'spirit'. The flesh wants the best of God on our terms, and Psalm 106:15 makes this point clear. It refers to Israel's desert journey when, after rejoicing in their freedom from slavery, they began to complain and crave for aspects of their old life. God then granted them their request but 'sent a wasting disease upon them'. God gave them the food they desired, but it brought leanness and not health. Their choice and request impacted their spiritual life, and spiritual leanness replaced spiritual health, losing their sense of privilege and blessing from belonging to God and dwelling in His Presence.

However, a hymn writer at the end of the nineteenth century saw through to the heart of the matter and gets us back on track.

Hymn by Frances Brook written in 1896
Her two sisters were missionaries, but she could not go because of ill-health. She penned this beautiful, inspiring hymn.

My goal is God Himself, not joy nor peace;
Nor even blessing, but Himself, my God:
'Tis His to lead me there, not mine but His –
At any cost, dear Lord, by any road!

Reflection point
The next phase of God's journey is a heart-searching one, asking us the question, 'How spiritual are you?' The Holy Spirit reveals the unspiritual aspects of our character, and also our need to increase our dependence on Him so that we follow in the footsteps of Jesus in life and ministry. Can the desire for successful and fruitful ministry be greater than the desire for God Himself?

CHAPTER 6

A heart pierced

When the people heard these distressing words, they began to mourn and no-one put on any ornaments. For the LORD had said to Moses, 'Tell the Israelites, "You are a stiff-necked people. If I were to go with you even for a moment, I might destroy you. Now take off your ornaments and I will decide what to do with you".' So the Israelites stripped off their ornaments at Mount Horeb. Now Moses used to take a tent and pitch it outside the camp some distance away, calling it the 'tent of meeting'. Anyone enquiring of the LORD would go to the tent of meeting outside the camp. And whenever Moses went out to the tent, all the people rose and stood at the entrances to their tents, watching Moses until he entered the tent. As Moses went into the tent, the pillar of cloud would come down and stay at the entrance, while the LORD spoke with Moses. Whenever the people saw the pillar of cloud standing at the entrance to the tent, they all stood and worshipped, each at the entrance to his tent. The LORD would speak to Moses face to face, as a man speaks with his friend. Then Moses would return to the camp, but his young assistant Joshua son of Nun did not leave the tent. (Exodus 33:4–11)

Yet now I am happy, not because you were made sorry, but because your sorrow led you to repentance. For you became sorrowful as God intended and so were not harmed in any way by us. (2 Corinthians 7:9)

The response of Moses and the people is the key that opens up God's way. It also meant God fulfilling His promises, and accompanying them with His Presence and Glory, moving them to the Promised Land.

In Exodus 33:4–11 we see three vital responses to God's challenge.

1. They began to mourn

Mourning is an expression of grief at a time of bereavement or repentance, in this case repentance. Repentance begins when we realise the consequences of our thoughts, words and actions to God and His Son. We have sinned against heaven and others, and this godly sorrow leads us to repentance (2 Corinthians 7:9). Repentance has been central to all movements of the Holy Spirit down through the ages.

It is a change of mind so that we think differently, accepting God's view of ourselves.

It is a change of heart so that Jesus becomes the new object of our love and loyalty and His interests become ours.

It is a change of direction, with the will turning its back on the self-centredness of sin and going God's way in obedience.

It is repentance from dead works (Hebrews 6:1 RSV). Dead works are activities without the life and breath of God.

At Pentecost, as Peter preached the Word, the Spirit moved powerfully, affecting some 3000 people deeply. Acts 2:37 says *'they were cut to the heart'*, that is acutely distressed, deeply upset to the point of being inconsolable apart from the mercy and grace of God.

The perception is that only really bad people need God's mercy. However, Jesus told a story of two people going into the temple to pray (Luke 18:9–14). The Pharisee said: *'I am glad I am not like other men, robbers, evildoers, adulterers or even like this tax-collector. I fast twice a week and give a tenth of all I have.'*

In the Kingdom of God we have no rights. We live by the mercy of God. When you see Jesus dying on the cross, redeeming our lives from the slave market of sin and rising from the dead, this is God's great and rich mercy shining at its brightest. Where does this leave us? Crying out like the tax-collector: 'Lord, be merciful to me a sinner.'

An ever-increasing understanding and experience of mercy leads us to an ever-increasing understanding and experience of grace. *'Let us then approach the throne of grace with confidence, so that we may receive mercy and find grace to help us in our time of need'* (Hebrews 4:16).

Peter writing towards the end of his life says: *'Praise be to the God and Father of our Lord Jesus Christ! In His great mercy He has given us new birth into a living hope through the resurrection of Jesus Christ from the dead'* (1 Peter 1:3).

After nearly 40 years of mission and ministry, I have to admit that in these last few years, as the Spirit of God has caused my heart to focus more and more on revival, He has led me to a deeper level of repentance.

When the Spirit of God shines into our hearts, in those special intimate moments, we find ourselves crying out like Isaiah, *'Woe is me!'* (Isaiah 6:5 RSV), and we begin to see things more clearly. We see the need to repent because we have fallen short of biblical patterns of life and ministry modelled by Jesus Himself. Often we prefer to hide in a place of safety, balance and personally constructed comfort zones. We realise that through Calvary we can have so much but we actually know so little, despite all our education and years as a Christian. Acknowledging that we profess much, we talk the talk, but possess so little, the demonstration aspect of life in the Spirit makes us feel very uncomfortable to the point of reluctance to be involved.

How can we be content with this?

When was the last time the Holy Spirit moved you to agonise and be distressed over your spiritual life, and then graciously led you to repentance?

When we compare ourselves to others, our lives do not look so bad. But when the Holy Spirit reveals that there is only one measurement standard, Jesus Christ, our hearts are broken and mourn in godly repentance.

Repentance, as I have mentioned, is also action. It never leaves you standing in the same place and repeating the same old words over again: that is more a response of self-pity. In repentance the Holy Spirit moves us first to be reconciled to God, and then to respond and be reconciled to man. The prime example of that in the New Testament is Zacchaeus in Luke 19:1–9. He stopped doing what he had become familiar with and was second nature to him, and started to do that which highlighted the new nature that salvation brings.

The exposure of Israel's heart in making a golden calf, and God's distressing words calling them 'a stiff-necked people' led them to mourn. We have been looking at this first response. As we come to the second response we see that their mourning or repentance led them into an action.

2. They did not put on their ornaments
The second of three things we notice about God's challenge to the Israelites in Exodus 33:4–11 is that they did not put on their ornaments.

Some commentators think that the earrings themselves were amulets, little idols worn as charms. This is altogether possible because many articles of jewellery were associated with idol worship (Isaiah 3:18–21).

We have already seen how, tired of waiting for Moses and anxious to have a visible god to go before them in the place of Moses' leadership, some of the Israelites brought their golden ornaments to Aaron. He used them to make a golden calf in imitation of the gods of Egypt (Exodus 32:2–4).

When the Israelites learned that God would no longer guide and protect them with His personal presence, they deeply repented of their transgression, *'and no one put on any ornaments'* (Exodus 33:4). Many have commented that the men were probably wearing armlets, bracelets and anklets like those worn by men in Egypt.

Relevance for today
I asked myself, 'What can we learn from this experience?' In referring specifically to the wilderness experience of the Israelites, Paul reminds us: *'These things happened to them as examples and were written down as warnings for us, on whom the fulfilment of the ages has come. So, if you*

think you are standing firm, be careful that you don't fall!' (1 Corinthians 10:11–12).

Like the Israelites of old, we desire to move forward on this next stage of God's journey. God's command to the Israelites is to remove their ornaments before going any further. If the wearing of ornaments contributed to the Israelites' rebellion against God and their removal facilitated reconciliation with God, could not the same be true for us today?

Ornaments may have a variety of meanings, and in themselves may not always be distractive or wrong. But as I reflected upon this in the context of Exodus 33:4–11, I sensed more and more the Spirit of God was giving me one aspect to emphasise, that of 'misplaced affections'. Excessive use can cause these ornaments to become like idols. They deflect us from God Himself, and the temptation to replace the centrality of God with lesser things is a constant temptation. They are misplaced because:

- they put you and me into the centre frame and not God Himself;
- they cause others to focus on our achievements and not God's glory;
- their purpose is to make you and me look more attractive and draw attention to ourselves;
- they focus on ministry trophies such as what we have done, where we have gone, the sacrifices we have made, the positions we have been given, and the acclaim and the praise of men we have received. All of this inflates the ego and causes the face of pride to shine.

If ever there was a time to remove these spiritual ornaments, it is now. *'I will not give my glory to another'* (Isaiah 42:8).

These misplaced affections are opposite to a lowly and contrite heart, a heart longing to be pure and holy before God. *'Who may ascend the hill of the LORD? Who may stand in his holy place? He who has clean hands and a pure heart, who does not lift up his soul to an idol or swear by what is false'* (Psalm 24:3–4).

Exodus 33:6 mentions that they stripped off their ornaments at Mount Horeb. Horeb means a place of dryness and desolation, or it could mean a place of the sword. It was a painful time. The writer to the Hebrews later wrote:

> *For the word of God is living and active. Sharper than any double-edged sword, it penetrates even to dividing soul and spirit, joints and marrow; it judges the thoughts and attitudes of the heart. Nothing in all creation is hidden from God's sight. Everything is uncovered and laid bare before the eyes of him to whom we must give account.* (Hebrews 4:12–13)

They suddenly realised the seriousness of their situation. As they thought about God not going with them, they could not get their ornaments off fast enough. This was a vigorous action brought about by their mourning. They realised in a fresh way their dryness and desperate need.

Let us fast-forward to Exodus 35:20–29:

> *Then the whole Israelite community withdrew from Moses' presence, and everyone who was willing and whose heart moved him came and brought an offering to the LORD for the work on the Tent of Meeting, for all its service, and for the sacred garments. All who were willing, men and women alike, came and*

*brought gold jewellery of all kinds: brooches, ear-
rings, rings and ornaments. They all presented their
gold as a wave offering to the LORD. Everyone who
had blue, purple or scarlet yarn or fine linen, or goat
hair, ram skins dyed red or hides of sea cows brought
them. Those presenting an offering of silver or bronze
brought it as an offering to the LORD, and everyone
who had acacia wood for any part of the work brought
it. Every skilled woman spun with her hands and
brought what she had spun – blue, purple or scarlet
yarn or fine linen. And all the women who were willing and had the skill spun the goat hair. The leaders
brought onyx stones and other gems to be mounted on
the ephod and breastpiece. They also brought spices
and olive oil for the light and for the anointing oil
and for the fragrant incense. All the Israelite men and
women who were willing brought to the LORD freewill
offerings for all the work the LORD through Moses had
commanded them to do.*

It is interesting to see the impact of internal revival. The
ornaments that were worn for personal attraction were
willingly given to the building of the Tabernacle. Hearts
were changed. The focus of attention was returning to
God Himself. The ornaments that were like a proud badge
covering the heart would now be donated completely to
the purposes of God.

3. Moses went into the Tent of the Meeting

The third thing to notice about God's challenge in Exodus
33:4–11 is that Moses went into the Tent of Meeting with
Joshua, his young assistant, while the people worshipped,
each at the entrance of their tent.

Surely this is the place that the Spirit of God will bring us to. This is the point of advance. Isn't this the whole thrust of Jehoshaphat's defeat of Moab and Ammon?

> *Jehoshaphat appointed men to sing to the LORD and to praise him for the splendour of his holiness as they went out at the head of the army, saying: 'Give thanks to the LORD, for his love endures for ever.'* (2 Chronicles 20:21)

Canaan represents so many mission opportunities, so many victories waiting to happen, so many unreached people longing to hear the Gospel. And yet, God's Spirit brings us to repent, to strip off our ornaments and find a new place of worship.

I have begun to realise that God's place of advance is so different from mine. Mine has been all too often action based and doing things, and yet here God is getting the heart of Moses and Israel to worship.

God is ready to move

And what happened when the Israelites repented? The pillar of cloud came down and stayed at the entrance of Moses' tent. God responds to repentance and a humbling of the heart before Him.

> *If my people, who are called by my name, will humble themselves and pray and seek my face and turn from their wicked ways, then will I hear from heaven and will forgive their sins and will heal their land. Now my eyes will be open and my ears attentive to the prayers offered in this place.* (2 Chronicles 7:14–15)

It is as if God is putting out the challenge to us: 'If you will humble yourselves, turn to me and seek my face. Then I will listen to your prayers and the cry of your heart.'

However, the appearance of God, whether in the cloud of His Presence or the revelation of Himself in any other way, always brings an awesome fear, causing men and women to tremble. But that trembling also carried a strong measure of relief that they had removed their ornaments and were on their faces before God. Just imagine the cloud of God's presence coming down and we are still wearing the ornaments of pride. What a scene of judgement!

The cloud was the means of leading His people forward; it was a sign of protection *but more than that* it revealed His glory and was a sign of His Presence. In the cloud of His Presence you rediscover the truth about God, His person and also His purposes.

So let's reflect again for a moment. It seems to me that God is preparing our hearts. He is speaking to us about the need for a supernatural moment with Him, the need for Him to catch our attention, challenging us to ask the question, 'If the old life reappeared what would it be for you and for me?'

Certainly for myself there are a number of things that immediately come to mind. Do I prefer to walk by sight and not by faith? Am I arranging ministry and future plans with the priority of pleasing myself and others who are close to me, and then asking God to bless it? How will I deal with the temptation to make things look better and more fruitful than they really are?

Then there are a whole host of attitudes which I can pretend do not affect me because I am supposed to be above them as a minister and missionary: envy, jealousy, anxiety, frustration, discontentment, unthankfulness, lack of self-control, a judgemental spirit. Though I may pretend

to be above it all, the only person I'm fooling is myself –
particularly concerning impatience and irritability!

Will our responses look like those of Moses, Joshua,
and the people in Exodus 33?

One final thought before we move on: *Just imagine the
cloud of God's presence coming down and we are still wearing the ornaments of pride.* What a scene of judgement!

---

*What will our choice be: a successful ministry directed
by an angel or the Presence of God?*

CHAPTER 7

Still more to understand

Hearts pierced by the Spirit gave this response:

- Moses, the senior leader, enquires of the Lord
- Joshua, the young assistant, just loved the Tent and the Presence and Glory of God
- The people stood and worshipped at the entrance of their tents.

The next part of God's preparation takes place in Exodus 33:12–23 and features a response from Moses and also from God.

> *Moses said to the LORD, 'You have been telling me, "Lead these people," but you have not let me know whom you will send with me. You have said, "I know you by name and you have found favour with me." If you are pleased with me, teach me your ways so I may know you and continue to find favour with you. Remember that this nation is your people.' The LORD replied, 'My Presence will go with you, and I will give you rest.' Then Moses said to him, 'If your Presence does not go with us, do not send us up from*

here. How will anyone know that you are pleased with me and with your people unless you go with us? What else will distinguish me and your people from all the other people on the face of the earth?' And the LORD said to Moses, 'I will do the very thing you have asked, because I am pleased with you and I know you by name.' Then Moses said, 'Now show me your glory.' And the LORD said, 'I will cause all my goodness to pass in front of you, and I will proclaim my name, the LORD, in your presence. I will have mercy on whom I will have mercy, and I will have compassion on whom I will have compassion.' But, he said, 'you cannot see my face, for no-one may see me and live'. Then the LORD said, 'There is a place near me where you may stand on a rock. When my glory passes by, I will put you in a cleft in the rock and cover you with my hand until I have passed by. Then I will remove my hand and you will my back; but my face must not be seen.'

We do not know exactly what took place when Moses entered the Tent of Meeting. Maybe in the back of his mind he was thinking of his earlier experience at the 'burning bush'. As the pillar of cloud came down he was once again standing on holy ground. The cloud symbolised God's revealed majesty, His awesome presence of holiness and power, and His tangible glory.

In this situation you don't get out your instruments or shout, praise and lift up your voice. You don't try to explain to God the place you are now in with its challenges, opportunities and threats. You certainly do not begin off-loading your ideas about the future ahead of you, what you want to do, where you want to go, or your plans and aspirations for ministry development and expansion.

What do you do? *You listen!* In verses 7–11 God is speaking to Moses face to face, and Moses is listening. How many times have I shared God's Word without first listening and hearing from Him?

Moses was called a prophet (Deuteronomy 34:10). Prophets were spokesmen of God, bringing vision to the believers and giving them a sense of purpose and direction through the living Word. The prophet's ministry is all about listening and seeing in the presence of God, and not primarily about speaking and doing.

Today this ministry is vital to keep us in contact with God and alive to the next stage of His journey for us. The prophet gives us an awareness of what God has and is doing in the world today. He brings the challenge to change the shape of our lives, churches and mission so as not to obscure the need of Jesus. He is not afraid to demonstrate God's feelings and passion and to ask searching questions that bring God back into the centre of our lives and ministry. He does this not just to humble us, necessary though that is, but to motivate us to press on.

I press on to take hold of that for which Christ Jesus took hold of me . . . I press on towards the goal to win the prize for which God has called me heavenwards in Christ Jesus. (Philippians 3:12–14)

If I may digress for a moment, I believe it is important to understand this. In order to catch our attention regarding the importance of listening, God uses silence.

God's purpose in silence

Facing people with deep needs is almost a daily experience in mission. This can be both heartbreaking and very stressful. Pressure to produce can be increased when God seems completely silent despite our fervent cries.

What do we do? Certainly handling people's expectations in their dire time of need has the potential of pushing us into dangerous territory, that of giving a word which comes out of the pressure of the occasion rather than the heart of God. Manufacturing a word – even out of compassion – can work against the purposes of God and be counterproductive.

Silence disciplines us. It tests our integrity and character. *Will we resist the great temptation to give a word we do not have?*

A secondary temptation can occur when our human compassion runs away with us and we add to what God is saying. This mostly takes place when prophecies are long. This is all part of God's refining and the continuing process of learning to walk with God. After all, let's be honest, whose voice do they really need to hear?

Isaiah and Jeremiah were both familiar with the challenge of God's silence. Today they warn us not to *'light your own fires'* (Isaiah 50:10–11) or *'speak a vision from our own minds'* (Jeremiah 23:16). It is one of the major ways that God tests and refines us.

> *As we read this passage Moses had both a question and a request.*

Question: 'Who will You send with me?'

Moses had been in the cloud of God's Presence, and yet he was struggling to put things together. 'This next stage of the journey is bigger than me; I need help. I am not as young as I was. These past 40 years have taken their toll.

I am not sure how much more I can take of leadership. This ministry has been heavy, wearing and lonely. Doesn't God understand my need for others to come alongside me?'

The revelation, as the presence and glory came down, was that one person with God is always a majority no matter how formidable the opposition may be or how daunting the next stage of the journey may seem. Loneliness and the feeling of isolation are often the burdens of a leader. The principle of the Kingdom of God, whether as seen through Esther in the Old Testament or in Acts in the New Testament, is that *'if God is for me who can be against me?'* (see Romans 8:31).

Of course God knew all Moses' needs as He does for all of us. After all, He is the God who knows when one hair falls from our head or one sparrow falls to the ground! God already had Moses' successor in mind, Joshua. You can't be anything but impressed with this young leader. This brave, courageous and proven warrior had one quality that far outweighed all others: he was a young man who loved to be in the Presence of God. Something in my heart leapt at this point. Can there be any better description of a leader's heart? All the training, all the equipping and all the potential hinges on this quality. The future of any church or mission organisation rests with a future leadership that models the heart of Joshua. And yet, reflecting upon times of leadership training and equipping, where is the longing for His Presence? How much time is spent discussing, planning, sharing about subject after subject, and how much time is spent longing for and seeking together His Presence?

At planning meetings and conferences we have our devotional times, messages, worship sessions and prayer moments, and these are important. But this level of determining to be in the presence of God and refusing anything less emanates not from a strategic mission or church manual but from a heart where the Holy Spirit is graciously ministering the pulse beat of God. It seems to me that 'catching the pulse beat of God's heart' was the issue that Moses was finding difficult to grasp, and perhaps we do too!

It was clear by God's response that Moses was missing the point. He was still thinking strategy, resources and how many leaders, etc. God speaks through all of his questioning, causing him to hear Him speak personally and powerfully: 'My Presence will go with you and I will give you rest' . . . isn't that enough?

Can you imagine the wonder of what God is communicating to Moses? Just think about it. Leading this many people into forbidding enemy territory with no fear, no anxiety, no insecurity, no sense of 'what on earth have I got myself into?' The amazing ability to rest even in the storm and battle of enemy territory is just amazing grace! Just like Jesus sleeping in the boat during the storm on the lake: He was resting in the security of His Father's love.

God's Presence does not mix with anxiety, stress or fear. We have pastoral ways of dealing with anxiety, stress, disappointment and everything else, which is commendable. I have met very few counsellors whose long-term remedy lies in the Presence of God. Perhaps this should be the first port of call and not a last resort?

In His Presence there is peace, fullness of joy, security, acceptance and total fulfilment.

It would seem at this point that the revelation of God is beginning to move the heart of Moses. It is the role of the Holy Spirit to illumine, to open our eyes:

Open my eyes that I may see wonderful things in your law. (Psalm 119:18)

I keep asking that the God of our Lord Jesus Christ, the glorious Father, may give you the Spirit of wisdom and revelation, so that you may know Him better. I pray also that the eyes of your heart may be enlightened in order that you may know the hope to which he has called you, the riches of his glorious inheritance in the saints . . . (Ephesians 1:17–18)

Revelation is light being shone into an otherwise dark world (Luke 2:32). It is God's gift uncovering our darkened understanding in order to know and experience divine truth. It is God communicating truth to the mind of man which he could not discover in any other way.

Blessed are you, Simon son of Jonah, for this was not revealed to you by man, but by my Father in heaven. (Matthew 16:17)

With this revelation touching Moses' heart we now see his continuing response in the form of a threefold request. This, I believe, comes directly out of this special moment in the Tent and there seems to me an order to these requests.

1. 'Teach me Your ways, so I may know You and continue to find favour with You.'

If this request is not high above those for success, multiplication of converts and churches, hitting goals, achieving vision, and financial provision, we may never grow into the second and third requests!

I wonder how many of us, over the years, have been so busy trying to work out our plans and mission field ministry that 'teach me your ways' is a secondary and not a primary request. Are we only praying this when we run out of ideas?

Brazil revisited

As the Holy Spirit impacted me with that prophecy of the jumbo jet full of God's new gifts, new supplies of His grace, love, freedom, revelation and truth and a fresh sense of His Presence and Glory, I found myself on my face before God.

For over two hours I wept before God, firstly for myself and my primary need to be taught, led and empowered by the Spirit of God, and then for those who I had the privilege of serving in Asia. It was both a chastening and cleansing moment of deep significance and an equipping moment. The verse from 2 Chronicles 7:14 echoed in my heart: *'If my people, who are called by my name, will humble themselves and pray and seek my face and turn from their wicked ways, then . . .'*

- I (God) will hear from heaven;
- I (God) will forgive their sin;
- I (God) will heal their land;
- I (God) will open my eyes and my ears to their prayers.

When we sincerely cry out, 'Teach me your ways', the Spirit of God is aroused and begins to stir something much deeper within us. We are consumed with being changed into His likeness and being in His Presence. At last we become aware that this is not another one-off event, but something that is both present and progressive. It is a dynamic and continuing work of the Spirit of God in me. It is not produced by effort and activity but is the gift of God's grace.

There are many reasons why a teachable spirit is so essential for the coming days of opportunity and advance. We need to ask ourselves a few questions:

Would we have chosen the route of the Red Sea to exit Egypt?

Would we not have just surrendered when Pharaoh's army was approaching and there was no escape?

Would we have chosen to cross the Jordan when its waters were at their highest and fiercest?

Would we have chosen the strategy of suggesting that the priests carry the Ark of the Covenant and walk into the river Jordan, with the belief that as soon as their feet touched the water a miracle would take place?

Would we have chosen to enter the land and face the seemingly impregnable city of Jericho?

Would we have chosen to walk and shout as the strategy to destroy the walls of Jericho?

Would we have chosen words of faith against the most modern weaponry of its day stored up by the enemy?

Of course not! Psalm 25:4–5 becomes a daily cry from our desperate hearts: *'Show me your ways, O LORD, teach me your paths; guide me in your truth and teach me, for you are God my Saviour, and my hope is in you all day long.'*

2. 'If your Presence does not go with us, do not send us up from here.'

Breakthrough at last. Moses' second request comes out of the first. He laid aside all the other thoughts and preferences that he had been holding to. In such an encounter the revelation of the Spirit bursts through all the fleshly expressions of our lives and ministries that had bound and restricted us for all too long. It is all about you, Lord.

The cries of John the Baptist, Jesus and Paul become ours: *'A voice of one crying in the desert, "Prepare the way for the Lord, make straight paths for Him" '* (Mark 1:3); *'You must increase and I must decrease'* (see John 3:30); *'By myself I can do nothing'* (John 5:30); *'I have been crucified with Christ and I no longer live, but Christ lives in me'* (Galatians 2:20).

My personal resurrection moment

It was Easter Sunday morning, 2010, and God woke me up at 4.30 am. I was aware that this moment was more than just me praising God and having a worship time and celebrating the wonder of the resurrection. The picture of the open grave was very graphic and I lay there in awe. Then the Holy Spirit spoke to my heart so clearly: 'It is time for you to come out of the grave and into resurrected life and ministry. I am rolling back the stone and calling you, like Lazarus, to come out.'

The words of Revelation 3:1 came forcefully to me: '*I know your deeds; you have a reputation of being alive, but you are dead.*' Could this apply to me, a missionary? I still rejoiced in the theological wonder of the resurrection as a foundation for my future hope. But from an experiential standing, in my current ministry, I desperately needed a fresh resurrection by the Spirit of God.

Prophetic challenge: 'Life in the tomb or life in the womb'

As I reflected further on the open grave, several thoughts began to emerge. For most of us in missions, the Apostle Paul is a central figurehead and example. In 1 Corinthians 15:31 he says, '*I die daily*' (KJV). Why would he say that? The answer is clear to me: so that he could be resurrected daily! This brought to mind the conflict so common to most of us, between resuscitation and resurrection.

Resuscitation is a request to God to do cosmetic surgery that will enable us to carry on respectfully in ministry. But that is not God's way. The more we desire this surface transformation the more our ministry reflects life in the tomb and not life in the womb of the Spirit.

The tomb can refer to:

- respectable Christian living
- a life that doesn't rock the boat, that keeps things neat and in order. We have today what is called 'messy church', but that is for kids not adults, right?
- where convenience is central and my desire to change is according to my preferences and what I think is appropriate, rather than God's will and purpose
- it is more to do with God doing things *for* me rather than *in* me
- it keeps relationships at arm's length and within the limits of my cultural acceptance
- it keeps ministry to that of pleasing man, operating at a level that is acceptable and proper
- it keeps life to a place where the praise of man is of greater pleasure and importance than the praise of God
- it is here that life and ministry become mechanical and theoretical, and where knowledge reigns but experience is left in the desert of emptiness
- the fruit of the Spirit is imprisoned within my cultural bounds and not the freedom of God
- the gifts of the Spirit are entombed within theological bounds; I can tell you what the gift of knowledge, prophecy or healing is all about but they are imprisoned in a tomb of understanding and no experience
- it leaves me aching for something to happen; frustrated and empty, where the Word is drying up. God's presence seems so distant . . .

God, I can't carry on like this! Will you please roll away the stone? I see now how selfish my request for resuscitation is. Will you please take my life out of the tomb and into the womb of the Spirit? Lord, resurrection! Lord, a new

Pentecost! Lord, a new day! A wineskin filled with the new wine of the Spirit! Lord, a new resurrected ministry that reflects Jesus and brings much fruit to the Father! *Lord, it is your Presence and Glory that I seek above all else.*

3. 'Show me your glory.'

This is Moses' final request of God. God's glory is something that belongs to Him alone. In John 17:5 Jesus talks about the glory He had with the Father before the world was made.

Hebrews 1:3 says that Jesus is the radiance of the Father's glory. Isaiah 43:7 tells us that we have been made to reflect God's glory. The brightness associated with His glory is the revelation of God Himself.

It was for this that we have been redeemed. The Spirit begins to shape us into the likeness of Christ and the glory impacts our relationships, our character, our ministry and acts of love and power.

Moses' plea to God to show him His glory was not a light-hearted moment of seeking signs and wonders for ministry success, but reflected Frances Brook's hymn: 'My goal is God Himself, not joy nor peace; nor even blessing, but Himself, my God.'

> *'It is time for you to come out of the grave and into resurrected life and ministry. I am rolling back the stone and calling you, like Lazarus, to come out.'*

Reflection point

As with the Israelites, God brings us to a decisive point – repentance that translates into a changed heart and mind and leads us to go God's way. Yes, ornaments removed, a new dimension of worship and obedience experienced. A new launching point that begins with waiting and listening in God's presence and moving at His command.

Now, almost ready to move on, there is one final aspect that needs to be firmly in place. Moses and the Israelites were now so aware of their unworthiness to be part of God's new tomorrow. Chapter Eight now brings us to the place of being impacted and amazed by the Goodness of God.

CHAPTER 8

The Goodness of God

*Then Moses said, 'Now how me your glory.' And the
LORD said, 'I will cause all my goodness to pass in front
of you, and I will proclaim my name, the LORD, in your
presence. I will have mercy on whom I will have mercy,
and I will have compassion on whom I will have compassion. But,' he said, 'you cannot see my face, for no-
one may see me and live.'* (Exodus 33:18–20)

How did God respond to Moses in Exodus 33:19? 'I will
cause all my goodness to pass in front of you.'

This surprised me at first. I had expected the thunder,
lightning and the dynamic physical evidence of God being
God. Perhaps an earthquake or at least another burning
bush experience. But it didn't happen like that. He caused
all His goodness to pass in front of Moses. Why?

I have tried to understand this and I find myself reflecting at a personal level. And perhaps this is what God
wanted Moses to do at this point. Is it possible that as the
years roll by the testimony of what God has done, both in
our personal and corporate lives, becomes so familiar that
it loses the wonder it once had? When asked to give our testimony, something inside us might say: 'Oh no, not again.'

The word 'goodness' means many things. The goodness
of God is that which disposes Him to be kind, benevolent,

and full of good-will; tender-hearted and with an unfailing attitude to be open, frank and friendly. By nature God loves to bless. He takes pleasure in blessing people. Goodness is the foundation stone that describes all that God is. It is the *drive* behind all the blessings He gives to us. Repentance is only possible because of God's goodness. Faith is simply confidence in the goodness of God. Holiness, justice, righteousness, love, power and all of God's attributes reflect His goodness.

> *The goodness of God is an infinite, overflowing fountain of understanding warmth, compassion and whole-heartedness!*

I wonder if in this moment two things occurred. First, Moses had a *review* of the goodness of God throughout his life:

- floating in a papyrus basket in a crocodile-infested Nile, how did he survive?
- the inexplicable way that Pharaoh's daughter had compassion on a Hebrew slave's child – and a boy at that! Surely he should have been killed?
- forty years on the run as a murderer and yet still in God's plan for tomorrow
- the amazing demonstration of God's power to Pharaoh and the Red Sea deliverance
- the provision in the wilderness of manna and quails and water from a rock
- the victory when Aaron and Hur lifted up his arms during the battle when the Amalekites were defeated
- meeting God at Mount Sinai, being given the Ten Commandments, the Tabernacle and the detailed revelation

regarding the Tabernacle? If Moses needed to see the 'goodness of God' once again, how much more do you and I? This experience would render him speechless and flat on his face before God. I know I wouldn't be any different.

My experience over the years confirms this truth. When the Spirit of God comes, He convicts me of sin, righteousness and judgement (John 16:8), and in that moment I feel totally unworthy, often in a place that seems to be opposite to the glory of God.

In this place what is my need? Surely it is to see the goodness of God? To know that the broken can be repaired, the lost can be found, the blind can see, those sitting in darkness can see a great light, grace and mercy mean the chains of yesterday can be broken, my future is not defined by my past and that this empty cup can be filled.

Whilst our superficial response may be 'I know all of that', maybe, deep in our heart, there is an awesome and eerie silence. We realise in a fresh and new way that the goodness of God opens the door of hope for tomorrow. And despite our spiritual bravado, in the deepest section of our heart there is a huge and sincere sigh of relief as mercy takes us into the throne room of God's grace once again. *'Let us then approach the throne of* grace *with confidence, so that we may receive* mercy *and find* grace *to help us in our time of need'* (Hebrews 4:16).

Secondly, in addition to a review of Moses' life in that moment, I wonder if he also had a *preview* that made Him realise He had experienced but a very pale reflection of the totality of who God really is.

Who among us would be so bold as to say we have got it all together, or that we are totally satisfied with our spiritual lives and the effectiveness of our ministry? The more the Word of God and the Spirit of God reveal the truth of God to our hearts, and the more time is spent in His Presence, the more we accept that there is so much more mercy and grace to receive because our sanctification is progressive, ongoing and far from complete. Whilst Paul calls the Corinthians 'saints', it refers not to character but to position: separated for God. Why is there a disconnect between what God has promised and what we experience in our daily lives? Paul gives us the answer in Galatians 5:17:

> *For the sinful nature desires what is contrary to the Spirit, and the Spirit what is contrary to the sinful nature. They are in conflict with each other, so that you do not do what you want.*

Hence the need to change and grow, and in that process we will experience new levels of mercy and grace.

The more the Word of God and the Spirit of God reveal the truth of God to our hearts, the more we are able to receive love, courage, faith and power. This is because there are different measures of faith. The Scriptures mention four:

- **Little faith** which focuses on circumstances more than God Himself as we find in Matthew 8:26. Or it focuses on the size of the opposition, as with Israel and the Philistines in 1 Samuel 17:11. Neither approach is able to see what the Spirit desires or just what God is able to do.
- **Faith devoid of action** which professes much and does very little. This is far distant from Jesus' example of 'doing' and 'teaching'. It was this that formed the heart of His teaching on the Kingdom to the disciples in Acts 1.
- **Faith that is strong** and believes in the promises of God no matter what people or circumstances may say.

But strong faith can still be improved, and this often through suffering. *'Consider it pure joy, my brothers, whenever you face trials of many kinds, because you know that the testing of your faith develops perseverance. Perseverance must finish its work so that you may be mature and complete, not lacking anything'* (James 1:2–4).

- Finally, **great faith** is that which believes God and His word when circumstances, emotions, appearances, people and human reason all seem to urge something to the contrary. This is exemplified by Job who, out of his hopelessness, darkness, pain and torment, cries out in Job 19:25–26: *'I know that my Redeemer lives, and that in the end he will stand upon the earth. And after my skin has been destroyed, yet in my flesh I will see God.'*

The more time we spend in His Presence, we will find that the Word and the Spirit will reveal to our hearts that there is so much more both to know and to experience of God Himself. We have mentioned a pivotal verse in this book, 2 Corinthians 3:18. Here Paul makes it clear that there are measures of glory. We will not be like Jesus until we see Him face to face. The measure of the Spirit we have received now will bear little resemblance to the measure of the Spirit we will receive when we become 'like Him'.

When God gives us a *preview* of the way ahead, primarily by showing His goodness, I believe it will leave us with an increased hunger and thirst for more of the Holy Spirit. What will this look like? Well, perhaps Luke 11:9–13 gives us a clue:

- 'ask' and keep on asking
- 'seek' and keep on seeking
- 'knock' and keep on knocking.

Why? There is always more of the Holy Spirit to receive and the Father longs to increase the manifestation of His love, joy and power to His children.

Finally, we accept that there is also a greater awareness of how much God hates sin but loves the sinner. History shows us the heart of God as He revives His people and prepares them for the next stage of His journey.

It is both the powerful presence of God and also the holiness of God that are central to transformation. The experience of revival is the experience of the Spirit of God, whose name is the Holy Spirit. The Spirit is holy and brings the holy character of God with him. And during times of revival when the Spirit is working, the holiness of God is very self-evident.

God's character is holy and righteous. It is as unlike ours as it can be. Yet another characteristic of God is that He wants our characters to be like His. So, whether God is active in the life of a single person or moving in a community, the Holy Spirit is radically changing people's hearts more and more into the likeness of God's righteousness, and translating that righteousness into altered behaviour patterns and transformed lives.

Holiness is positive

How often we regard 'holiness' as no more than a string of negative ideas full of no-go areas, no-go habits and no-go people! The word 'holiness' needs to be redeemed and restored to its real, biblical meaning. It needs to be seen as something glorious: the expression of God's own character, with which He endows us as He gives us His Spirit. God is holy, and is in the process of making us like Himself and making us to reflect His glory. Holiness exposes unholy acts. God is giving us the capacity to be like Him in character, in power, in creativity, in lifestyle and in all things! And that is really positive because holiness exposes unholy acts and attitudes. When God's holy character is reproduced in us, the Holy Spirit cleans up our minds and habits, and changes our behaviour and disposition. When this transforming power begins to affect the outside world as well, we see an upturn in the whole moral climate. This changes lives both in the church and in society.

The goodness of God becomes clear in Exodus 34:10:

I am making a covenant with you. Before all your people I will do wonders never before done in any nation in all the world. The people you live among will see how awesome is the work that I, the LORD, will do for you.

Moses had a fresh glimpse of the glory and presence of God, and received the promise of seeing wonders greater than anyone had witnessed before.

As much as many of us have been praying for, longing for, and dreaming of a divine moment when the presence and glory of God are evident in revival, this whole sequence of events in Exodus 32 and 33 makes me reflect that the primary 'wow' of that moment is once again godly fear.

It has been said that the greatness of God rouses fear within us. That is the testimony of those who have lived in revival times. As mentioned earlier, the cry of Isaiah typifies the response, even of the godliest, when in the presence of God we cry, 'Woe is me'.

The goodness of God encourages us not to be afraid but to ascend the hill of the Lord and to taste and see that the Lord is good.

O God, my hope, my heavenly rest,
My all of happiness below,
Grant my importunate request
To me, to me, Thy goodness show;
Before my faith's enlightened eyes,
Make all thy gracious goodness pass;
Thy goodness is the sight I prize:
O might I see thy smiling face:
Reveal thy love, thy glorious name.

(Charles Wesley)

CHAPTER 9

No more wandering in the desert

What I have shared in this book is not the product of study so much as an opening of my heart to what God has personally been doing in me over these last few years.

I know that God has done so much in my own sphere at WEC International, Betel and so many other missions and churches worldwide. Nobody would discount the miracle of God's intervention worldwide and the faith and courage of known and unknown saints who have laid down their lives for the Gospel.

However, these are incredibly challenging days, while also full of unbelievable opportunity. In this respect, there is a parallel with Moses and the people who were on the edge of entering Canaan: so near and yet so far!

In the introduction I said that there is so much more to God, and I wonder whether you and I will be part of discovering and experiencing that truth. As I finish, I find this question is still in the forefront of my mind.

My longing is that we will see the Spirit of God poured out in revival and the world reached with the Gospel of Jesus Christ in both word and deed.

Even though I have only touched on a few issues particularly relevant to all of us at this time, we will need to:

- recognise that our gifting, though important, will never be sufficient in itself to complete God's journey and finish His task;
- see our desperate need of a fresh encounter with God by the Spirit;
- allow God to get our attention through whatever means He chooses, and bring us back to His agenda and purpose;
- open our lives to the Holy Spirit, so He can rid us of our 'golden calves' and 'ornaments';
- welcome the cleansing work of the Word and the Spirit, and in particular be aware of how the seemingly little and insignificant (impatience and irritability) can derail and corrupt;
- respond with repentance that leads to action and change, and enter into a new place of worship;
- refuse to kindle our own flame, and learn to wait on God even when He is silent;
- seek a deeper understanding and awareness of the goodness of God.

Shantung revival of 1932

There is one more story I wish to share with you. It is from China and the Shantung revival of 1932. What does it look like when the presence and glory of God comes? Of course no one story can ever depict the indescribable glory of God, but this just opened my eyes a little more and created a hunger and thirst to know God in a new way.

Twenty missionaries and friends gathered to pray for the serious eye condition of Mrs. Culpepper, a missionary for many years in China. After two hours of earnest prayer, Dr. Culpepper anointed his wife and prayed for her eyes. Suddenly it was as though God had walked into the room. Everyone prayed aloud and it was as if heaven had come down.

Two Chinese cooks known for their mutual hatred walked into the room. They were gripped by the convicting power of the Spirit, confessed their hatred of each other, sought forgiveness and were gloriously saved. Suddenly someone said to Mrs. Culpepper, 'What about your eyes?' She had been completely healed.

This was the prelude, just the beginning and the first drop of heavenly rain in the Shantung Revival. Yes, there were many signs, wonders and healings, but these were overshadowed by the greatest revelation of all: Jesus Christ as both Saviour and Lord.

The challenge of Exodus 32 and 33 brings us to a similar point. God longed to move Israel into Canaan, and today God longs to see the world come to know His Son Jesus.

There is no better way for me to end than with the threefold request of Moses:

'Teach me Your ways'
    'Lord, if your Presence does not go with us, we are not moving'
    'Show me Your Glory.'

The world is waiting; the fields are ripe for harvest, but God's question remains:

How much do you really desire My Presence and My Glory? Will you leave the desert . . . with Me?